1

Fire is for cooking food. Fire is used for getting warm. The First People had fire to cook and keep warm.

3

Fire will burn grass. The grass will grow again. The grass will have green leaves. Animals love green grass.

How did the First People make fire? They carried fire sticks. If there were no fire sticks what did they do? They had to make fire from dry wood and leaves.

7

The end of the stick was kept dry. This end would heat up when spun in a hole. This would make heat and smoke.

9

To make fire you need a dry stick. The stick would go into the groove. This would be spun very fast. This would make heat and smoke.

11

When the stick is spun it gives off smoke. The heat can start to burn wood. Small bits of dry leaves are used. This starts a little fire. The fire is put under some leaves to make it burn.

The fire starts very small. Twigs and leaves are used. This makes the fire hot. Slowly add big pieces of wood.

15

Some wood is slow to burn. The best wood is from gum trees. Gum tree wood burns very hot. Some wood is smoky and does not make a hot fire.

17

Dry wood was burned. The fire was used to keep warm and cook food. Meat would be put on the fire and cooked. Seeds and fruits were also cooked in the ashes.

19

The fire will burn all night keeping people warm. People would sleep close to the fire. The sticks will still burn for the next night.

21

Food could be cooked among stones. It was buried with hot ash and sand on top. The food would cook slowly.

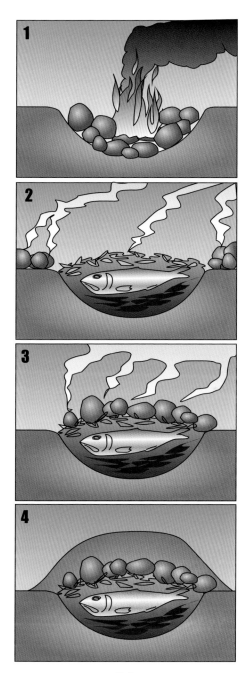

23

Word bank

cooking

warm

leaves

smoke

stick

twigs

pieces

smoky

slowly

stones

twine

scrape

flakes.